Unicorn Gratitude Journal

FOR KIDS

Daily Writing Prompts for Girls
100 Days!

©2019 Annie's Notebooks
All Rights Reserved. Art is original or under license.

This book belongs to...

_____

Date: _____

Today I am grateful for…

_____
_____
_____
_____
_____
_____
_____
_____

My favorite thing that happened today:

_____
_____
_____
_____
_____
_____
_____

Today, I feel…

Date: _____

Today I am grateful for…

_____
_____
_____
_____
_____
_____
_____
_____

My favorite thing that happened today:

_____
_____
_____
_____
_____
_____
_____

Today, I feel…

Date: _____

Today I am grateful for…

_____
_____
_____
_____
_____
_____
_____

My favorite thing that happened today:

_____
_____
_____
_____
_____
_____
_____

Today, I feel…

Date: _____

Today I am grateful for...

_____
_____
_____
_____
_____
_____
_____
_____

My favorite thing that happened today:

_____
_____
_____
_____
_____
_____
_____

Today, I feel...

Date: _____

Today I am grateful for…

_____
_____
_____
_____
_____
_____
_____
_____

My favorite thing that happened today:

_____
_____
_____
_____
_____
_____
_____

Today, I feel…

Date: _____

Today I am grateful for...

_____
_____
_____
_____
_____
_____
_____
_____

My favorite thing that happened today:

_____
_____
_____
_____
_____
_____
_____

Today, I feel...

Date: _____

Today I am grateful for…

_____
_____
_____
_____
_____
_____
_____
_____

My favorite thing that happened today:

_____
_____
_____
_____
_____
_____
_____

Today, I feel…

Date: _____

Today I am grateful for...

_____
_____
_____
_____
_____
_____
_____
_____

My favorite thing that happened today:

_____
_____
_____
_____
_____
_____
_____

Today, I feel...

Date: _____

Today I am grateful for…

_____
_____
_____
_____
_____
_____
_____
_____

My favorite thing that happened today:

_____
_____
_____
_____
_____
_____
_____

Today, I feel…

Date: _____

Today I am grateful for…

_____
_____
_____
_____
_____
_____
_____
_____

My favorite thing that happened today:

_____
_____
_____
_____
_____
_____
_____

Today, I feel…

Date: _____

Today I am grateful for...

_____
_____
_____
_____
_____
_____
_____
_____

My favorite thing that happened today:

_____
_____
_____
_____
_____
_____
_____

Today, I feel...

Date: _____

Today I am grateful for…

_____
_____
_____
_____
_____
_____
_____
_____

My favorite thing that happened today:

_____
_____
_____
_____
_____
_____

Today, I feel…

Date: _____

Today I am grateful for…

_____
_____
_____
_____
_____
_____
_____
_____

My favorite thing that happened today:

_____
_____
_____
_____
_____
_____
_____

Today, I feel…

Date: _____

Today I am grateful for…

_____
_____
_____
_____
_____
_____
_____
_____

My favorite thing that happened today:

_____
_____
_____
_____
_____
_____
_____
_____

Today, I feel…

Date: _____

Today I am grateful for…

_____
_____
_____
_____
_____
_____
_____
_____

My favorite thing that happened today:

_____
_____
_____
_____
_____
_____
_____

Today, I feel…

Date: _____

Today I am grateful for...

_____
_____
_____
_____
_____
_____
_____
_____
_____

My favorite thing that happened today:

_____
_____
_____
_____
_____
_____
_____

Today, I feel...

Date: _____

Today I am grateful for...

_____
_____
_____
_____
_____
_____
_____
_____

My favorite thing that happened today:

_____
_____
_____
_____
_____
_____
_____

Today, I feel...

Date: _____

Today I am grateful for...

_____
_____
_____
_____
_____
_____
_____
_____

My favorite thing that happened today:

_____
_____
_____
_____
_____
_____
_____
_____

Today, I feel...

Date: _____

Today I am grateful for…

_____
_____
_____
_____
_____
_____
_____
_____

My favorite thing that happened today:

_____
_____
_____
_____
_____
_____
_____

Today, I feel…

Date: _____

Today I am grateful for…

_____
_____
_____
_____
_____
_____
_____
_____

My favorite thing that happened today:

_____
_____
_____
_____
_____
_____
_____

Today, I feel…

Date: _____

Today I am grateful for…

_____
_____
_____
_____
_____
_____
_____
_____

My favorite thing that happened today:

_____
_____
_____
_____
_____
_____
_____

Today, I feel…

Date: _____

Today I am grateful for…

_____
_____
_____
_____
_____
_____
_____
_____

My favorite thing that happened today:

_____
_____
_____
_____
_____
_____
_____

Today, I feel…

Date: _____

Today I am grateful for...

_____
_____
_____
_____
_____
_____
_____
_____

My favorite thing that happened today:

_____
_____
_____
_____
_____
_____
_____

Today, I feel...

Date: _____

Today I am grateful for...

_____
_____
_____
_____
_____
_____
_____
_____
_____

My favorite thing that happened today:

_____
_____
_____
_____
_____
_____
_____

Today, I feel...

Date: _____

Today I am grateful for…

_____
_____
_____
_____
_____
_____
_____
_____

My favorite thing that happened today:

_____
_____
_____
_____
_____
_____

Today, I feel…

Date: _____

Today I am grateful for...

_____
_____
_____
_____
_____
_____
_____
_____

My favorite thing that happened today:

_____
_____
_____
_____
_____
_____
_____

Today, I feel...

Date: _____

Today I am grateful for…

_____
_____
_____
_____
_____
_____
_____
_____

My favorite thing that happened today:

_____
_____
_____
_____
_____
_____
_____
_____

Today, I feel…

Date: _____

Today I am grateful for…

_____
_____
_____
_____
_____
_____
_____
_____

My favorite thing that happened today:

_____
_____
_____
_____
_____
_____
_____

Today, I feel…

Date: _____

Today I am grateful for…

_____
_____
_____
_____
_____
_____
_____

My favorite thing that happened today:

_____
_____
_____
_____
_____
_____

Today, I feel…

Date: _____

Today I am grateful for...

_____
_____
_____
_____
_____
_____
_____
_____

My favorite thing that happened today:

_____
_____
_____
_____
_____
_____
_____

Today, I feel...

Date: _____

Today I am grateful for…

_____
_____
_____
_____
_____
_____
_____
_____

My favorite thing that happened today:

_____
_____
_____
_____
_____
_____
_____

Today, I feel…

Date: _____

Today I am grateful for…

_____
_____
_____
_____
_____
_____
_____
_____

My favorite thing that happened today:

_____
_____
_____
_____
_____
_____
_____

Today, I feel…

Date: _____

Today I am grateful for…

_____
_____
_____
_____
_____
_____
_____
_____

My favorite thing that happened today:

_____
_____
_____
_____
_____
_____
_____

Today, I feel…

Date: _____

Today I am grateful for…

_____
_____
_____
_____
_____
_____
_____
_____

My favorite thing that happened today:

_____
_____
_____
_____
_____
_____
_____

Today, I feel…

Date: _____

Today I am grateful for…

_____
_____
_____
_____
_____
_____
_____

My favorite thing that happened today:

_____
_____
_____
_____
_____
_____
_____

Today, I feel…

Date: _____

Today I am grateful for…

_____
_____
_____
_____
_____
_____
_____
_____
_____

My favorite thing that happened today:

_____
_____
_____
_____
_____
_____
_____

Today, I feel…   😎 🙂 😐 🙁 ☹️

Date: _____

Today I am grateful for…

_____
_____
_____
_____
_____
_____
_____

My favorite thing that happened today:

_____
_____
_____
_____
_____
_____
_____

Today, I feel…

Date: _____

Today I am grateful for…

_____
_____
_____
_____
_____
_____
_____
_____

My favorite thing that happened today:

_____
_____
_____
_____
_____
_____
_____
_____

Today, I feel…

Date: _____

Today I am grateful for…

_____
_____
_____
_____
_____
_____
_____
_____

My favorite thing that happened today:

_____
_____
_____
_____
_____
_____
_____

Today, I feel…

Date: _____

Today I am grateful for...

_____
_____
_____
_____
_____
_____
_____
_____

My favorite thing that happened today:

_____
_____
_____
_____
_____
_____
_____

Today, I feel...

Date: _____

Today I am grateful for...

_____
_____
_____
_____
_____
_____
_____

My favorite thing that happened today:

_____
_____
_____
_____
_____
_____
_____

Today, I feel...

Date: _____

Today I am grateful for…

_____
_____
_____
_____
_____
_____
_____
_____

My favorite thing that happened today:

_____
_____
_____
_____
_____
_____
_____

Today, I feel…

Date: _____

Today I am grateful for…

_____
_____
_____
_____
_____
_____
_____
_____

My favorite thing that happened today:

_____
_____
_____
_____
_____
_____
_____

Today, I feel…

Date: _____

Today I am grateful for…

_____
_____
_____
_____
_____
_____
_____
_____

My favorite thing that happened today:

_____
_____
_____
_____
_____
_____
_____

Today, I feel…

Date: _____

Today I am grateful for…

_____
_____
_____
_____
_____
_____
_____
_____

My favorite thing that happened today:

_____
_____
_____
_____
_____
_____
_____

Today, I feel…

Date: _____

Today I am grateful for…

_____
_____
_____
_____
_____
_____
_____
_____
_____

My favorite thing that happened today:

_____
_____
_____
_____
_____
_____
_____
_____

Today, I feel…

Date: _____

Today I am grateful for...

_____
_____
_____
_____
_____
_____
_____
_____

My favorite thing that happened today:

_____
_____
_____
_____
_____
_____
_____

Today, I feel...

Date: _____

Today I am grateful for...

_____
_____
_____
_____
_____
_____
_____
_____

My favorite thing that happened today:

_____
_____
_____
_____
_____
_____
_____

Today, I feel...

Date: _____

Today I am grateful for…

_____
_____
_____
_____
_____
_____
_____
_____

My favorite thing that happened today:

_____
_____
_____
_____
_____
_____
_____

Today, I feel…

Date: _____

Today I am grateful for…

_____
_____
_____
_____
_____
_____
_____
_____

My favorite thing that happened today:

_____
_____
_____
_____
_____
_____
_____

Today, I feel…

Date: _____

Today I am grateful for…

_____
_____
_____
_____
_____
_____
_____
_____

My favorite thing that happened today:

_____
_____
_____
_____
_____
_____
_____
_____

Today, I feel…

Date: _____

Today I am grateful for…

_____
_____
_____
_____
_____
_____
_____
_____

My favorite thing that happened today:

_____
_____
_____
_____
_____
_____
_____

Today, I feel…

Date: _____

Today I am grateful for...

_____
_____
_____
_____
_____
_____
_____

My favorite thing that happened today:

_____
_____
_____
_____
_____
_____
_____

Today, I feel...

Date: _____

Today I am grateful for...

_____
_____
_____
_____
_____
_____
_____
_____

My favorite thing that happened today:

_____
_____
_____
_____
_____
_____
_____

Today, I feel...

Date: _____

Today I am grateful for…

_____
_____
_____
_____
_____
_____
_____
_____

My favorite thing that happened today:

_____
_____
_____
_____
_____
_____
_____

Today, I feel…

Date: _____

Today I am grateful for…

_____
_____
_____
_____
_____
_____
_____
_____

My favorite thing that happened today:

_____
_____
_____
_____
_____
_____
_____

Today, I feel…

Date: _____

Today I am grateful for…

_____
_____
_____
_____
_____
_____
_____
_____

My favorite thing that happened today:

_____
_____
_____
_____
_____
_____
_____

Today, I feel…

Date: _____

Today I am grateful for…

_____
_____
_____
_____
_____
_____
_____
_____

My favorite thing that happened today:

_____
_____
_____
_____
_____
_____
_____

Today, I feel…

Date: _____

Today I am grateful for…

_____
_____
_____
_____
_____
_____
_____
_____

My favorite thing that happened today:

_____
_____
_____
_____
_____
_____
_____

Today, I feel…

Date: _____

Today I am grateful for…

_____
_____
_____
_____
_____
_____
_____
_____

My favorite thing that happened today:

_____
_____
_____
_____
_____
_____
_____

Today, I feel…

Date: _____

Today I am grateful for…

_____
_____
_____
_____
_____
_____
_____

My favorite thing that happened today:

_____
_____
_____
_____
_____
_____

Today, I feel…

Date: _____

Today I am grateful for…

_____
_____
_____
_____
_____
_____
_____
_____
_____

My favorite thing that happened today:

_____
_____
_____
_____
_____
_____
_____

Today, I feel…

Date: _____

Today I am grateful for…

_____
_____
_____
_____
_____
_____
_____
_____

My favorite thing that happened today:

_____
_____
_____
_____
_____
_____
_____

Today, I feel…

Date: _____

Today I am grateful for...

_____
_____
_____
_____
_____
_____
_____
_____

My favorite thing that happened today:

_____
_____
_____
_____
_____
_____
_____

Today, I feel...

Date: _____

Today I am grateful for...

_____
_____
_____
_____
_____
_____
_____
_____

My favorite thing that happened today:

_____
_____
_____
_____
_____
_____
_____

Today, I feel...

Date: _____

Today I am grateful for...

_____
_____
_____
_____
_____
_____
_____
_____

My favorite thing that happened today:

_____
_____
_____
_____
_____
_____

Today, I feel...

Date: _____

Today I am grateful for…

_____
_____
_____
_____
_____
_____
_____
_____

My favorite thing that happened today:

_____
_____
_____
_____
_____
_____
_____

Today, I feel…

Date: _____

Today I am grateful for...

_____
_____
_____
_____
_____
_____
_____
_____

My favorite thing that happened today:

_____
_____
_____
_____
_____
_____
_____

Today, I feel...

Date: _____

Today I am grateful for…

_____
_____
_____
_____
_____
_____
_____
_____

My favorite thing that happened today:

_____
_____
_____
_____
_____
_____
_____

Today, I feel…

Date: _____

Today I am grateful for…

_____
_____
_____
_____
_____
_____
_____
_____

My favorite thing that happened today:

_____
_____
_____
_____
_____
_____
_____

Today, I feel…

Date: _____

Today I am grateful for...

_____
_____
_____
_____
_____
_____
_____
_____

My favorite thing that happened today:

_____
_____
_____
_____
_____
_____
_____
_____

Today, I feel...

Date: _____

Today I am grateful for…

_____
_____
_____
_____
_____
_____
_____
_____

My favorite thing that happened today:

_____
_____
_____
_____
_____
_____
_____

Today, I feel…

Date: _____

Today I am grateful for…

_____
_____
_____
_____
_____
_____
_____
_____

My favorite thing that happened today:

_____
_____
_____
_____
_____
_____
_____

Today, I feel…

Date: _____

Today I am grateful for…

_____
_____
_____
_____
_____
_____
_____
_____

My favorite thing that happened today:

_____
_____
_____
_____
_____
_____

Today, I feel…   😎 🙂 😐 🙁 ☹️

Date: _____

Today I am grateful for...

_____
_____
_____
_____
_____
_____
_____
_____

My favorite thing that happened today:

_____
_____
_____
_____
_____
_____
_____

Today, I feel...

Date: _____

Today I am grateful for…

_____
_____
_____
_____
_____
_____
_____
_____

My favorite thing that happened today:

_____
_____
_____
_____
_____
_____
_____

Today, I feel…

Date: _____

Today I am grateful for...

_____
_____
_____
_____
_____
_____
_____
_____

My favorite thing that happened today:

_____
_____
_____
_____
_____
_____
_____

Today, I feel...

Date: _____

Today I am grateful for…

_____
_____
_____
_____
_____
_____
_____
_____

My favorite thing that happened today:

_____
_____
_____
_____
_____
_____
_____

Today, I feel…

Date: _____

Today I am grateful for…

_____
_____
_____
_____
_____
_____
_____
_____

My favorite thing that happened today:

_____
_____
_____
_____
_____
_____
_____
_____

Today, I feel…

Date: _____

Today I am grateful for…

_____
_____
_____
_____
_____
_____
_____
_____

My favorite thing that happened today:

_____
_____
_____
_____
_____
_____
_____

Today, I feel…

Date: _____

Today I am grateful for…

_____
_____
_____
_____
_____
_____
_____
_____

My favorite thing that happened today:

_____
_____
_____
_____
_____
_____
_____

Today, I feel…

Date: _____

Today I am grateful for...

_____
_____
_____
_____
_____
_____
_____
_____

My favorite thing that happened today:

_____
_____
_____
_____
_____
_____
_____

Today, I feel...

Date: _____

Today I am grateful for…

_____
_____
_____
_____
_____
_____
_____
_____

My favorite thing that happened today:

_____
_____
_____
_____
_____
_____
_____

Today, I feel…

Date: _____

Today I am grateful for…

_____
_____
_____
_____
_____
_____
_____
_____

My favorite thing that happened today:

_____
_____
_____
_____
_____
_____
_____

Today, I feel…

Date: _____

Today I am grateful for…

_____
_____
_____
_____
_____
_____
_____

My favorite thing that happened today:

_____
_____
_____
_____
_____
_____
_____

Today, I feel…

Date: _____

Today I am grateful for...

_____
_____
_____
_____
_____
_____
_____
_____

My favorite thing that happened today:

_____
_____
_____
_____
_____
_____
_____

Today, I feel...

Date: _____

Today I am grateful for...

_____
_____
_____
_____
_____
_____
_____
_____

My favorite thing that happened today:

_____
_____
_____
_____
_____
_____
_____

Today, I feel...

Date: _____

Today I am grateful for…

_____
_____
_____
_____
_____
_____
_____
_____

My favorite thing that happened today:

_____
_____
_____
_____
_____
_____
_____

Today, I feel…

Date: _____

Today I am grateful for...

_____
_____
_____
_____
_____
_____
_____
_____

My favorite thing that happened today:

_____
_____
_____
_____
_____
_____
_____

Today, I feel...

Date: _____

Today I am grateful for…

_____
_____
_____
_____
_____
_____
_____
_____

My favorite thing that happened today:

_____
_____
_____
_____
_____
_____
_____

Today, I feel…

Date: _____

Today I am grateful for…

_____
_____
_____
_____
_____
_____
_____
_____

My favorite thing that happened today:

_____
_____
_____
_____
_____
_____
_____

Today, I feel…

Date: _____

Today I am grateful for…

_____
_____
_____
_____
_____
_____
_____
_____

My favorite thing that happened today:

_____
_____
_____
_____
_____
_____
_____

Today, I feel…

Date: _____

Today I am grateful for…

_____
_____
_____
_____
_____
_____
_____
_____

My favorite thing that happened today:

_____
_____
_____
_____
_____
_____
_____

Today, I feel…

Date: _____

Today I am grateful for...

_____
_____
_____
_____
_____
_____
_____

My favorite thing that happened today:

_____
_____
_____
_____
_____
_____

Today, I feel...

Date: _____

Today I am grateful for…

_____
_____
_____
_____
_____
_____
_____
_____

My favorite thing that happened today:

_____
_____
_____
_____
_____
_____
_____

Today, I feel…

Date: _____

Today I am grateful for…

_____
_____
_____
_____
_____
_____
_____
_____

My favorite thing that happened today:

_____
_____
_____
_____
_____
_____
_____

Today, I feel…

Date: _____

Today I am grateful for…

_____
_____
_____
_____
_____
_____
_____

My favorite thing that happened today:

_____
_____
_____
_____
_____
_____

Today, I feel…

Date: _____

Today I am grateful for…

_____
_____
_____
_____
_____
_____
_____
_____

My favorite thing that happened today:

_____
_____
_____
_____
_____
_____
_____

Today, I feel…

Date: _____

Today I am grateful for...

_____
_____
_____
_____
_____
_____
_____
_____

My favorite thing that happened today:

_____
_____
_____
_____
_____
_____
_____

Today, I feel...

Date: _____

Today I am grateful for...

_____
_____
_____
_____
_____
_____
_____
_____

My favorite thing that happened today:

_____
_____
_____
_____
_____
_____
_____

Today, I feel...

Date: _____

Today I am grateful for…

_____
_____
_____
_____
_____
_____
_____
_____

My favorite thing that happened today:

_____
_____
_____
_____
_____
_____
_____

Today, I feel…

Date: _____

Today I am grateful for...

_____
_____
_____
_____
_____
_____
_____
_____

My favorite thing that happened today:

_____
_____
_____
_____
_____
_____
_____

Today, I feel...

Date: _____

Today I am grateful for...

_____
_____
_____
_____
_____
_____
_____
_____

My favorite thing that happened today:

_____
_____
_____
_____
_____
_____
_____
_____

Today, I feel...

Date: _____

Today I am grateful for...

_____
_____
_____
_____
_____
_____
_____
_____

My favorite thing that happened today:

_____
_____
_____
_____
_____
_____
_____

Today, I feel...

**If you've enjoyed this book,
please leave me a review on Amazon :)**

–Annie's Notebooks